ABSOLUT.®
COCKTAILS

Absolut Vodka Drinks for Every Occasion

Hardie Grant

QUADRILLE

CONTENTS

THE
ABSOLUT
STORY

THE SPIRIT OF CULTURE

Watch a film or pick up a book, and the stories that unfold are rarely sparked by someone eating a salad; instead great stories, plot twists and turns, times of pure entertainment and light-bulb moments often have cocktails at the heart of them. The history of cocktails is ultimately the history of how people interact; they add that little something to moments of joyful connection and help those moments live on well beyond the last sip.

Absolut Vodka has more than its fair share of stories: iconic moments of human connection that have become folklore over the ages and earned a place in culture.

Legend has it that Andy Warhol spotted a bottle of Absolut Vodka across the bar at the world-famous 1970s New York nightclub, Studio 54. He was seduced by its apothecary-inspired bottle in the same way that other items in the grocery cart had caught his attention a decade before. This chance sighting inspired a long creative partnership with the brand; amusingly, rumour has it that Andy even chose to wear Absolut as a perfume.

The brand became iconic, as did the cocktails made with Absolut. The Cosmopolitan came into being in the early 1980s, but only really surged in popularity when it made its debut in the second episode of *Sex and the City*. It became *the* drink to be seen with and, over time, also proved to be a turning point in culture. The Cosmopolitan was deliberately chosen for being pretty, pink and glamorous, while maintaining an air of being just out of reach and intrinsically aspirational. It's important to remember that, even as recently as the late 90s, the notion of successful, unattached, thirty-something women running around the city sipping cocktails and doing whatever they wanted was revolutionary.

While there are cocktails that endure — classics with timeless qualities — others are created on the spot to meet the mood and needs of a moment in time. In the haze of one of the big fashion weeks in the 1980s, a young model (allegedly now world famous) put a barman to the test with an unusual request. A combination of vodka, fresh espresso, coffee liqueur and sugar was shaken into a frothy delight we now get to ask for by name: the Espresso Martini.

Absolut was not just part of culture, but also helped shape it through boldness and creativity. Creativity flows through everything from the design of its bottle to its advertising campaigns, collaborations with artists, fashion designers and musicians, and ultimately, into the drinks themselves. This creativity is still present in everything the brand does, in a way that feels uniquely Absolut.

Over the next few pages, we are going to dip into some of our favourite stories, little snippets from the past for you to serve up alongside lip-smackingly good cocktails.

BORN TO BE DIFFERENT

We already know the bottle was an attention grabber; here's why.

Compared to other bottles on the market at the time in the late 70s/early 80s, it was a total game changer: transparent and inspired by an 18th-century medicine bottle, it stood out a mile from its tall, flashy competitors.

It was a design that not everyone was quick to appreciate, and it bombed in consumer research. The focus groups all fed back negatively: 'you can't see the name of the product', 'you don't know what it is', 'it looks like an IV bottle turned over, you think you're in hospital'.

The neck was considered too short, the shoulders bulged out, and it was produced (and still is today) in Åhus, a small village in southern Sweden. The only 'vodka' country at the time was Russia, a few domestically made brands and a very small number of Eastern European vodkas. Compared to these, Absolut looked, tasted and behaved differently. Launched at the high end of the market at a time when the concept of 'premium white spirits' simply didn't exist, Absolut broke the codes of the category in more ways than one and went on to become an icon of creativity.

This legacy of 'doing things differently' has stuck with the brand to this very day, a pioneering spirit that still guides its actions and behaviour.

GAME-CHANGING ADVERTISING

By 1980, it was clear that Absolut Vodka was here to stay, and that a new premium vodka category had been born. While Absolut had successfully launched in bars in New York, it still needed to branch out and reach consumers globally.

Absolut briefed New York based advertising agency TBWA to create a campaign, and it soon became clear that not just any campaign would do.

"Some of the most iconic advertising campaigns in history have come from turning a weakness at product level into a selling point. Absolut was facing exactly that challenge when it decided to market itself beyond Sweden. As a colourless, odourless spirit from the wrong country and in a funny shaped bottle, it needed something extra special. Together with advertising agency TBWA, Absolut turned these perceived weaknesses into strengths, something that was only made possible by being entirely true to the brand." Says Tad Greenough, Global Chief Creative Officer.

Absolut Perfection, Absolut's first commercial, was launched in 1981 and went on to become one of the longest-running advertising campaigns in history.

Where other brands created loud, abrasive campaigns, this one was true to its Scandinavian roots — cool, sophisticated and always with the iconic bottle front and centre. Simple imagery combined with a single-minded message delivered a promise of purity and never-seen-before quality, a game changer for the category.

The launch of Absolut Perfection was revolutionary, and sparked a 25-year-long campaign that included about 2000 ads.

ABSOLUT CLARITY.

ABSOLUT ATTRACTION.

ABSOLUT MAGNETISM.

ABSOLUT BRAVO.

Every print ad was centred around the bottle and an ever-changing line: 'Absolut...'. It showed a witty perspective of the world through an Absolut lens, a versatile view that could lean into any scene, trend, or moment of cultural relevance.

In the mid 80s, Absolut launched the 'city series' — a series of bespoke campaigns created to explore a connection with a local audience. Each one featured a bottle representative of something the city is famous for.

The campaign was instantly recognisable, with an appeal that sometimes went just a little too far. The story goes, as Absolut advertisements began to blow up in the 80s, they gave US libraries quite a headache: waves of enthusiasts ripped up the library stock of magazines, tearing out the ads to include them in their personal collections.

ABSOLUT L.A.

ABSOLUT ROME.

ABSOLUT EDINBURGH.

ABSOLUT GENEVA.

ABSOLUT NEW ORLEANS.

ABSOLUT VODKA IS THE SUPREME CHOICE ANYWHERE IN THE WORLD.
ENJOYED NEAT, ON THE ROCKS, OR IN DRINKS AND COCKTAILS.

ABSOLUT MONTE CARLO.

ABSOLUT ATHENS.

ABSOLUT CHICAGO.

ABSOLUT. THERE IS NO PURER VODKA. DRINK IT NEAT AT 0°C. IT WILL BLOW YOU AWAY.

ABSOLUT IN ART, FASHION, MUSIC & BEYOND

The first Absolut collaboration was in 1985, when Andy Warhol met with Michel Roux, the man charged with launching the brand in the US market. The artist told him, 'I love the bottle. I'd love to do something'.

He was the first artist to express his creative vision through the Absolut bottle shape, which kickstarted and inspired a lifetime of collaborations with other members of the creative community we now recognise for their contributions towards shaping the culture of the time. What started as a small group of up-and-coming artists soon swelled to an expansive collective whose collaborations went well beyond art and traditional genres.

In 1988, Absolut exploded into the fashion world with the now famous dress by designer David Cameron which everyone seemed to want: the brand received about 5,000 calls a day from people hoping to purchase it.

Crossovers with all creative forms in culture soon followed: music, fashion and film all provided opportunities for the brand to transcend visual art and explore other areas. Artists, fashion designers and musicians were given the chance to push well beyond their usual confines and express themselves in a broader, more accessible and democratic space, showing Absolut's true strength as a cultural provocateur and multiplier.

PRETTY WITH A PURPOSE

It was only a matter of time before the Absolut creativity spilled over onto the bottle in a way that wasn't 'art for art's sake', but instead something with a clear purpose.

From the very beginning, Absolut mixed queer culture with popular culture through fashion, art and nightlife. Instinctively, it knew that this made things more interesting, and pioneered greater diversity and inclusivity long before it was culturally acceptable to do so.

In the early 1980s, most brands didn't dare to advertise in gay magazines for fear that it would damage their reputation. Absolut did the opposite, and did it with enormous pride.

One of Absolut's limited edition bottles, the Absolut No Label, challenged prejudices about sexual identity by stripping the bottle of all logos to show that outside appearance shouldn't overshadow what's inside. Another, the Absolut Colors bottle, created in 2008 in collaboration with artist Gilbert Baker — designer of the original rainbow flag back in 1978 — was the first spirit bottle to bear the pride flag, something Absolut continues to produce in updated designs to this day.

Since the first limited edition bottle came out in 2002, hundreds have been produced. While the bottles themselves are without a doubt things of beauty, the sentiment behind them is perhaps even more compelling, as they tackle social issues head-on. To this day, Absolut's limited edition bottles still drive positive change by encouraging conversation in the real world.

Absolut Colors 2008 limited edition bottle photographed by Absolut Regis

—

THE WORLD'S LARGEST COMMUNITY MADE VODKA

Vodka has been the number-one spirit on the global market for a very long time. Even now, while upstarts such as tequila and gin dance onto the scene, vodka still dominates. Why? Because vodka allows for limitless creativity; its versatility makes it an unstoppable force. And when it comes to Absolut Vodka, it has things that make it, well, Absolut.

In the 19th century, the Swedish industrialist and politician L.O. Smith was one of the most famous people in the country. Today, we know him as the man on the medallion of the Absolut Vodka bottles.

L.O. Smith was the first person in Sweden to introduce a new method for purifying vodka on a large scale. He wanted to get rid of the unpleasant-tasting and unhealthy fusel alcohol and instead offer an absolutely pure vodka. He introduced continuous distillation to Sweden and in 1879 he created the 'Absolut Rent Brännvin' (which translates as 'absolutely pure vodka'), an idea that would eventually grow into what we now know as Absolut Vodka. Over 150 years later, Absolut is still using this method and doesn't just distil once, twice or even eight times. Instead, it is continuously distilled — to perfection.

Continuous distillation is not the only thing that makes Absolut different. It took a leaf out of wine production's book, meaning where provenance, growing conditions, and climate are all valued for their impact on the quality and character of the raw ingredients.

Unlike most vodka brands, Absolut Vodka is only produced in one place: Åhus, a small village in southern Sweden. To this day, the brand has kept true to its 'village mentality', and all the ingredients used in the production process still come from in and around southern Sweden, produced by the local community. When we say, 'all the ingredients', we only really mean two: winter wheat and pristine water. The water comes from local wells that are up to 200m deep, and has been filtered through Swedish bedrock for thousands of years.

Absolut is very particular about its wheat. It has to be winter wheat — nothing else will do — and it has to come from the region of Skåne in the south of Sweden, where it's grown by local farmers Absolut knows by name, who deliver it directly to the one and only distillery — which is where the real magic happens.

And the magic is in the details: Absolut controls the end-to-end production process from the moment the wheat is harvested to when the vodka is finally bottled and packed. This 'seed to bottle' process is the brand's quality guarantee, and this is how it can be entirely sure that every bottle of Absolut Vodka tastes exactly as it should: smooth and crisp, with hints of vanilla and caramel.

To make Absolut, it takes real expertise and a deep understanding of all the aspects of the production process. Often, this knowledge is passed on from one generation of workers to the next in ways that go way beyond the training manual. This knowledge is so precious for those who have it that they are not allowed to travel together in the same plane.

The community of people Absolut depends on to produce its vodka is so critically important that it is embedded in its production philosophy, along with where it comes from, and what it is made of: 'One Source, One Community'.

The 'One Source, One Community' commitment matters because you can actually taste it in Absolut's vodka, wherever you are in the world. The truth is, whether you are in Buenos Aires or London, every single bottle of Absolut was born in the small village of Åhus.

Because great-tasting vodka is so dependent on the natural riches the world has to offer, Absolut has always been extra mindful of what it uses and what it puts back into the world. The brand's journey towards becoming one of the world's most energy-efficient distilleries started over three decades ago.

Back then, sustainability was far from a buzzword, and something that neither marketers nor investors paid that much attention to, but Absolut invested heavily as early as 1990 in ways to save energy. It was simply a question of common sense.

In 1996, Absolut invested in a new spirit distillation process, with a view to increasing the amount of vodka it could produce without increasing its energy consumption. Within four years, it had reduced its energy consumption by half again. Today, more than 85 per cent of the energy Absolut uses at its production sites comes from renewable sources.[1]

Absolut's carbon footprint has also been a key focus for the brand. The Absolut distillery has been net carbon neutral since 2013, and for those who really want the nitty gritty detail, the product carbon footprint of a 70cl or 75cl Absolut bottle is 1.1kg CO_2e/l vodka.[2]

[1] Sources:
- Sweden, Åhus, Köpmannagatan - Environment & Bottling, 2020, 2021 and 2022 reports
- Sweden, Åhus - Satellite - Environment & Bottling 2020, 2021 and 2022 reports
- Sweden Nobbelov Distillery - Environment Distillery, 2020, 2021 and 2022 reports
· Vattenkraft EPD®, Hydropower electricity report for the May 1st, 2019 – December 31st, 2022 period

[2] Source: Life cycle assessment of the greenhouse gas emissions caused by the life cycle of Absolut Vodka report, DGE Sweden & Absolut Vodka, 2022

BORN TO MIX

So, why does how a vodka is made matter? Honestly, it's because you get to taste it in every sip. The better the vodka, the better the cocktail. And good cocktails make people happy in ways that beer and wine simply can't.

Cocktails transport you somewhere else; they are a little firework in a glass, an explosive mix of flavours and sensations that make new memories and elicit old ones, with great stories along the way.

Why we drink cocktails doesn't tend to change much, but *what* we drink evolves as tastes and fashions change over time. Modern cocktail trends have revealed a classic cocktail revival as we pucker up for more sours and welcome the return of the 'tini' with open arms. Today, we are perhaps a little less fussy and a little more tuned in. So quality over quantity.

Cocktails are more than a drink; they are a mood, a language in themselves, and they come in so many shapes, sizes, colours, textures and tastes. In the same way that you may want a bacon sandwich one day and a lobster bisque the next, the never-ending possibilities mean that you can create something that works for you, right now. And this is what this book is here to do: it's the ultimate guide for great vodka cocktails that are right for every occasion, taste and mood.

Planning a big night in? This book has statement cocktails that dazzle and impress. And 'impress' does not have to mean you are chained to the kitchen sink — we have some sneaky little hacks so you get all the glory and none of the pain.

For something more casual and easy-going, opt for fruity little numbers, like the Raspberri Sunrise (page 118) or the Pineapple Martini (page 126) or a classic, like the Black Russian (page 92).

The Summer Sippers section will convince even the most resistant to broaden out from beer for that sun-kissed barbecue you are planning. And there are solutions to lift every event — from Valentine's Day to Halloween — with something special.

'Special' does not have to mean difficult; making a cocktail is not a dark arts or something only the 'chosen ones' can do. You don't need a fully equipped professional bar; instead, you'll find some new uses for egg cups and mason jars that are already in the cupboard.

The truth is, everyone can mix a drink, and there isn't just one way to do it, either. So get mixing, share some old stories, and create some new ones.

TECHNIQUES

Shaking There are two types of shaking: the wet shake and the dry shake. The wet shake is the default assumed in this book, unless stated otherwise. It does three things to a cocktail: it mixes ingredients together, chills them to an appealingly drinkable temperature, and adds a little bit of dilution. Pack a Boston shaker (page 30) full of ice, put the two parts together and shake vigorously in a long motion until chilled. The dry shake, which is used less often than the wet, is done without ice, either before or after the wet shake. Its purpose is to emulsify, whip or foam a cocktail when it includes ingredients such as egg white or aquafaba — imagine making a meringue.

Zesting and Twisting When choosing a citrus to zest, go for a fruit with a thick peel — it'll produce more oil. Use a vegetable peeler (page 30) or knife to cut off a long, thick strip of zest, but leave behind the fruit flesh and as much white pith as possible. Then, without wasting any time, twist it directly over the drink to release those fresh, intense oils. Lemon, lime and orange are the most popular zests for cocktails.

Muddling A cocktail-maker's term for 'mashing'. Put the ingredients to be muddled in a shaker or glass, then gently crush them using a muddler (page 32) — or a pestle, or thin rolling pin, or anything that'll fit, really.

Straining and double-straining After shaking, split the shaker into two parts, leaving the ice and cocktail in one side. Place a hawthorn strainer (page 30) over the top and use it to hold back the ice and other solids while letting the delicious liquids flow into your glass. To double-strain, do the same but hold a fine strainer (page 30) above the glass for extra filtering.

Rimming Take two saucers. Put some water (or citrus, when called for) in one, and the rim ingredient in the other (cinnamon, chocolate, salt, etc). Gently rub the rim of the glass in the liquid then in the rim ingredient. Beautiful.

Stirring A gentler way of mixing a drink than shaking, and done when less dilution is needed. Make sure your long bar spoon (page 30) reaches the bottom of the glass, and stir in a circular motion until chilled. Clockwise or anticlockwise? Now, that's up to you.

Building drinks With some cocktails, neither shaking nor stirring is necessary — ingredients can be simply poured into the glass, usually over ice.

Rolling Somewhere between shaking and stirring, rolling is a technique that chills, aerates and provides minor dilution — but without any bashing. Put your ingredients in one side of the shaker, and fill the other with ice. Pour between the two sides about five or six times, before straining liquids into a glass, neat or over fresh ice.

Infusing vodka You'll need a bottle of Absolut Original and a sealable jar big enough to hold all the liquid and ingredients. Mix them together and leave for the instructed time — this could range from a few minutes to 24 hours, although some more subtle flavours can be infused for seven days.

EQUIPMENT

When you walk into a bar and see the array of fancy equipment the bartenders have at their disposal, you might think: leave the cocktail making to the experts. But we're here to tell you that mixing drinks doesn't have to be complicated. Even with a few bits and pieces you've probably got in your kitchen, you can make drinks that'll impress your friends to no end. We do still think that a couple of choice pieces of equipment will make life a lot easier, so if you want to take your home bar set-up to the next level, we've recommended some here. Don't be intimidated by making cocktails at home — you've got this.

1. Shaker Probably the most important piece of equipment the home bartender needs. Shakers do three things: mix ingredients together, chill the ingredients, and dilute them a little if ice is involved. Our favourite is a Boston shaker, which comes in two parts. Don't worry if you don't have a Boston shaker, though — home alternatives include a mason jar, or any clean jar with a lid.

2. Strainer Used to hold back ice and other solids after shaking, while letting the good stuff pour out. The pro bartender's version has a little handle and spring, and is called a 'hawthorn' strainer. At home, you could also use a pasta strainer, or a mason jar with the lid covering most of the opening — anything that allows the liquid out and keeps ice and other chunky bits in.

3. Fine strainer Basically a mini sieve. Used along with a regular strainer, it removes all ice particles and pesky bits of fruit that could get stuck in your teeth. A smooth drink guaranteed.

4. Bar spoon An extra-long utensil with a thin handle for superior stirring. Don't have a bar spoon handy? Try a chopstick or any other long, thin utensil.

5. Peeler For those long, juicy strips of citrus zest, you need a Y-shaped peeler. A sharp knife works too, but make sure to trim the white bits off.

—

1

2

3

4

5

6

7

8

9

10

6. Blender Essential for frozen drinks, bringing a creamy, smooth and slush texture. We recommend an electric stand mixer over a stick blender — they're easier and cleaner.

7. Juicer A centrifugal juicer extracts juice at a super-high speed, resulting in what we call aeration: basically a fluffy, frothy texture in the drink. It makes the job of juicing citrus, pineapple and other fruits easy-peasy. Don't have a centrifugal juicer? No worries — while it won't give this fluffy texture, a regular press or juicer will extract juices just fine. The most important thing is to use the best possible ingredients in your drinks — it makes a big difference — and nothing beats freshly squeezed juice!

8. Jigger Aka a measure — it ensures you're putting accurate volumes of ingredients into your cocktails to get the balance just right. Being able to follow a recipe's measurements accurately is the best way to ensure a delicious result, but if needed you can go by proportions of ingredients using a shot glass, egg cup or baking spoon instead.

9. Mixing glass For those 'stirred, not shaken' moments, a large beaker-shaped glass for packing full of ice and stirring down strong or neat mixes. This will chill, dilute a little, and mix all the ingredients. If you don't have a mixing glass, any large glass, small vase, mason jar or tall mixing bowl will work too.

10. Muddler Like a pestle, the bartender uses a muddler to mash (or 'muddle') soft ingredients, like fruit or herbs, to extract flavour. An easy alternative could be a small rolling pin or masher.

SYRUPS

Simple Syrup This is something every bar must have! Make it at home by heating equal parts caster sugar and water over a low heat until the sugar is completely dissolved. Let it cool, and pour into bottles or some other lidded vessel that is easy to use. You can store it in the fridge for around 1 month.

Rich Syrup A rich syrup simply means using more sugar than a simple syrup. It's made in the same way as a simple syrup, but with two parts caster sugar to one part water. It will keep in the fridge for up to 6 months.

Vanilla Syrup To make vanilla syrup follow the recipe for simple syrup then, once the sugar is completely dissolved and you remove your pan from the heat, add pure vanilla extract, stir and let the syrup cool. You will want to add 1 tablespoon of vanilla extra per 500ml of simple syrup. Store in the fridge for up to 2 weeks.

GRENADINE

2 Large **Pomegranates** (or 2 Cups **Pomegranate Juice**)
450g **Caster Sugar**
60g **Pomegranate Molasses**
1 teaspoon **Orange Blossom Water**
30ml **Absolut Vodka** (optional)

Cut the pomegranates in half and juice using a citrus press. (This should yield about 2 cups of juice or use two cups high-quality bottled pomegranate juice.) Pour the pomegranate juice into a large glass, measuring cup or other microwave-safe container and microwave at full power for 1–2 minutes until warm. Add the sugar and stir until it dissolves completely, then add the pomegranate molasses and orange blossom water and stir to combine. Allow to cool, then transfer to a bottle. Add the vodka as a preservative, if you like.

GLASSES

1. Highball Tall and skinny, this reduces the surface area of long drinks, keeping them fizzy and cold for longer. Any tall tumbler or collins glass is a good alternative.

2. Martini The classic Y-shaped glass with a long stem to reduce heat transfer from hands to the glass. The steeply sloped sides prevent ingredients from separating and allow garnishes on toothpicks to stay upright.

3. Rocks or Lowball For short drinks served — you guessed it — on the rocks (in other words, over ice). This glass can also be used for sipping spirits.

4. Shot The smallest glass packs the biggest punch. Used for party-starting flavour bombs and typically holds around 30–60ml.

5. Wine Okay, it's obvious — a wine glass is for wine, but its wide bowl and long stem make it a great vessel for light, summery drinks like spritzes and coolers as well.

6. Sundae Just as the sundae glass makes ice cream ten times more appealing, it does the same with the right cocktail. Think big, tall, tiki-style drinks like the Monday in Marrakech (page 140).

7. Coupe Another stemmed glass for neat drinks, often used interchangeably with the martini glass. The coupe has seen a rise in popularity due to its elegant saucer design and practicality as its content is less likely to spill over the edge than in a martini glass.

8. Champagne As elegant as the sparkling that's served in it, champagne glasses (aka flutes or tulips) add a similar sophistication to straight-up, effervescent cocktails. Its tall and narrow shape has a purpose — it retains champagne's signature carbonation by reducing the surface area for it to escape.

1   2   3   4

5   6   7   8

COCKTAILS
TO
IMPRESS

COSMOPOLITAN

This blushingly pink cocktail was given A-list status by a certain NYC-based sitcom — it might be a 90s icon, but it's no throwback. It's all about the balance here, with the fresh taste of Absolut Citron and lime matching the sweetness of the triple sec and cranberry juice. You'll want to perfect the flaming zest technique for extra kudos, so practise beforehand.

Ice Cubes
40ml **Absolut Citron**
20ml **Triple Sec**
20ml **Lime Juice**
20ml **Cranberry Juice**
1 Twist **Orange Zest**

Start by filling a shaker with ice cubes, then add the Absolut Citron, triple sec, lime juice and cranberry juice, and shake vigorously. Strain into a cocktail glass, then twist a piece of orange zest over the drink so that all the delicious oils spray onto the surface. Drop the garnish in as the final touch.

HOW-TO-MIX VIDEO

LONG ISLAND ICED TEA

Five spirits, plus a lick of cola and a measure of lemon to make the drink last longer — layers upon layers of flavours with a kick. In 1972, a well-known newspaper called the Long Island Iced Tea 'the Unofficial Drink of Summer', which sums it up very well — this drink has been starting parties for decades. Easy to make, easy to drink.

Ice Cubes
20ml **Absolut Vodka**
20ml **Light Rum**
20ml **Gin**
20ml **Tequila Blanco**
20ml **Triple Sec**
40ml **Lemon Juice**
20ml **Cola**
1 Wheel **Lemon**

Fill a highball glass with ice, then add all the ingredients except the cola and lemon wheel, then give it a good stir. Top with the cola, garnish with a lemon wheel, kick back and get sipping!

HOW-TO-MIX VIDEO

ESPRESSO MARTINI

This is one of the most knockout drinks you can make at home. Trends come and go in the cocktail world, but the Espresso Martini seems to never go out of fashion — and it's everywhere right now. Could be because of the rich coffee taste, could be because of the beautiful cream created by the shaking, could be because the ultra-photogenic layers add a 'wow' moment. A modern classic.

Ice Cubes
45ml **Absolut Vodka**
25ml **Kahlúa**
25ml **Espresso**
3 Whole **Coffee Beans**

Fill a cocktail shaker with ice. Add the vodka, Kahlúa and espresso before giving it a good shake. The more you shake, the more impressive the frothy cream head on the drink. Strain into a cocktail or martini glass. Garnish with three coffee beans, which are said to represent health, wealth and happiness.

HOW-TO-MIX VIDEO

SEX ON THE BEACH

A proper fun-times drink with a sweet fruitiness that tastes like a holiday in a glass, even if it's winter outside. This is one that looks as good as it tastes.

Ice Cubes
20ml **Absolut Vodka**
100ml **Light Orange Juice**
20ml **Peach Schnapps**
100ml **Cranberry Juice**
1 Wheel **Lime**
1 Whole **Cherry**

Add plenty of ice to a highball glass and pour in all the liquid ingredients to make this classic. Garnish with the lime, and put a cherry on top. Literally...

HOW-TO-MIX VIDEO

PORNSTAR MARTINI

The smooth taste of vanilla in the vodka elevates the sharp, tropical sweetness of the passion fruit to create a hedonistic classic that's become one of the most popular cocktails in the UK. Often served with a shot of champagne on the side to balance the sweetness in the cocktail and take the sense of celebration up a level.

2.5cm Thick Slice **Pineapple**
45ml **Absolut Vanilia**
15ml **Vanilla Syrup**
25ml **Passion Fruit Purée**
1 **Passion Fruit**
Ice Cubes
Champagne or sparkling wine

Start by muddling the pineapple in a shaker. Add the Absolut Vanilia, vanilla syrup and passion fruit purée, followed by the ice. Shake it like you mean it, then double-strain into a chilled cocktail glass. Garnish with half a passion fruit and serve with a shot of ice-cold Champagne.

HOW-TO-MIX VIDEO

STRAWBERRY NIGHT

Absolut Vanilia, with its rich, creamy notes, is the perfect companion to apple, passion fruit and strawberry, which is what makes this fruit-first cocktail so luscious. Think of this as a liquid dessert — and you don't just have to serve it after dinner.

3–4 **Strawberries**
10ml **Simple Syrup**
Ice Cubes
30ml **Absolut Vanilia**
20ml **Lemon Juice**
35ml **Passion Fruit Juice** or **Tropical Juice**
20ml **Passion Fruit Liqueur**
1 Wedge **Pineapple**

Cut the strawberries into pieces and add to a shaker with the simple syrup. Muddle. Then add ice to the shaker and pour in the rest of the liquid ingredients. Give it a good shake to mix well and get it ice cold before straining into a highball glass filled with ice cubes. For a final touch, garnish with a pineapple wedge.

LYCHEE MARTINI

Unmistakably delicate, perfumed lychee is amplified by the smooth, clean Absolut Vodka — this is a one-on-one combo that gives both ingredients the freedom to express themselves. The result is candied and sweet but alcohol forward. Sometimes a cocktail doesn't need anything else.

Ice Cubes
45ml **Absolut Vodka**
15ml **Lychee Liqueur**
1 Whole, Peeled **Lychee**

Fill a mixing glass with ice cubes, then add the vodka and lychee liqueur. Give it a good stir to combine beautifully and get it nice and cold. Strain into a martini glass or coupe and garnish with a lychee for that finishing touch.

HOW-TO-MIX VIDEO

CITRON GIMLET

A bona fide classic, the Gimlet has stood the test of time — and with good reason. It was first drunk by British Navy officers on long voyages, just for the vitamin C, of course. The Gimlet flourished in the 20th-century golden age of the cocktail, and it's still here today. The original recipe uses gin, but here the zestiness of the Absolut Citron scythes through the sweetness of the simple syrup to create something special.

Ice Cubes
45ml **Absolut Citron**
25ml **Simple Syrup**
25ml **Lime Juice**
1 Twist **Lime Zest**

This is an easy one: fill a rocks glass with ice cubes, then pour in the Absolut Citron, simple syrup and lime juice. Give it a quick stir before garnishing with a lime zest twist.

FANCY NANCY

Orange, orange and orange: the Fancy Nancy puts the fruit in the spotlight, but it's not just one note. The bitter Italian liqueur, sweet triple sec and freshly squeezed orange itself are enhanced by the Absolut Vodka. Let it sing!

Ice Cubes
30ml **Absolut Vodka**
10ml **Campari**
45ml **Orange Juice**
15ml **Triple Sec**
10ml **Simple Syrup**
1 Twist **Orange Zest**

Add plenty of ice to a shaker and pour in all the liquid ingredients. Give it a really good shake to get it nice and cold, before double-straining into a cocktail glass. Garnish with an orange zest twist. So simple, but so good.

VODKA MARTINI

Vodka sometimes gets called a neutral spirit, but that's not the whole story. Mix up a Vodka Martini and let the slight caramel and vanilla hints of Absolut shine through, followed by its fresh and fruity finish. Unveil a few of these at your party, and watch it get a whole lot more sophisticated.

Ice Cubes
45ml **Absolut Vodka**
5ml **Dry Vermouth**
1 Twist **Lemon Zest**
1 Whole **Green Olive**

Fill a mixing glass with ice cubes, then pour in the vodka and vermouth and stir until perfectly chilled. Strain into a cocktail glass before twisting a piece of lemon zest over the drink, making sure all the delicious oils land on the surface. Garnish with the twisted lemon zest and a green olive.

HOW-TO-MIX VIDEO

BLUE HAWAIIAN

Ask any bartender to tell you a secret, and they'll say they love making blue drinks. Okay, maybe they're not cool, sophisticated or 'craft', but they are a whole lot of fun, and nothing brings the kitschy tiki vibes like a blended blue cocktail. The Blue Hawaiian is a modernised version of the 1950s classic Blue Hawaii, and it's so evocative you can practically hear the steel guitar notes drifting among the palm trees.

Ice Cubes
25ml **Absolut Vodka**
25ml **Blue Curaçao**
10ml **Coconut Syrup**
Pineapple Juice
1 Whole **Cherry**

Fill a highball glass with ice cubes, then add the vodka, blue curaçao and coconut syrup. Give it a stir before topping up with pineapple juice. Garnish with a cherry on top.

SIT DOWN

A very spirit-forward drink with the vivid, freshly squeezed flavour of Absolut Lime and the bitter, herby digestif Amaro Ramazzotti. Fix yourself a Sit Down, sit down somewhere comfortable and settle in.

Ice Cubes
20ml **Calvados**
20ml **Amaro Ramazzotti**
40ml **Absolut Lime**
1 Twist **Lime Zest**

Fill a mixing glass with ice cubes, then pour in the calvados, Amaro Ramazzotti and Absolut Lime. Stir well and get the ingredients deliciously cold before straining into a cocktail glass. For a final touch, garnish with a lime zest twist.

HOW-TO-MIX VIDEO

MUDSLIDE

Like dessert, coffee and digestif all rolled into one, the Mudslide is a sweet, creamy, boozy treat. You might have seen the frozen, blended version on menus, but we reckon this shaken one is a classy way to round off a dinner party.

Ice Cubes
25ml **Absolut Vodka**
25ml **Cream Liqueur**
25ml **Kahlúa**

Fill a shaker with ice cubes and pour in the vodka, cream liqueur and Kahlúa. Shake until deliciously chilled before straining into a rocks glass filled with ice cubes.

BLUSHING BRIDE

No need to wait until a wedding to mix up this one. It's a glorious marriage between Absolut vodka and cherry liqueur, uplifted by some punchy citrus. The egg white becomes delightfully fluffy when shaken — don't be tempted to miss it out.

Ice Cubes
30ml **Absolut Vodka**
10ml **Cherry Liqueur**
10ml **Egg White**
20ml **Lime Juice**
10ml **Orange Curaçao**
10ml **Simple Syrup**

This recipe needs a double shake: first, add all the ingredients to a shaker with ice, then give it a good shake to chill and combine flavours. Strain to remove the ice, then return it to the shaker without ice and go again to get your egg whites nice and fluffy. Pour into a cocktail or martini glass and enjoy.
It's so worth the effort.

GANGSTER

Like the Vodka Martini (page 56), this is a drink that makes the most of the balanced, harmonious characteristics of Absolut Vodka. The name is a tribute to the Absolut creator, the Swedish spirits maker Lars Olsson Smith: a true pioneer and the man on the seal of our bottle.

Ice Cubes
5ml **Rich Syrup**
12ml **Lillet Blanc**
4 Dshes **Clove Bitters**
45ml **Absolut Vodka**
1 Twist **Orange Zest**

Fill a mixing glass with ice cubes and pour in all the liquid ingredients. Stir until nice and chilled, then strain into a rocks glass filled with chunky ice cubes. Garnish with an orange zest twist for that final touch.

HOW-TO-MIX VIDEO

LEMON DROP SHOT

Here's a shot that's lively, sweet and zesty all at once — a tray of these is a great way to kick off a party. The sugared rim is a special little touch that elevates a tray of Lemon Drops way above a straightforward poured-out shot.

1 Wedge **Lemon**
Caster Sugar
Ice Cubes
20ml **Absolut Citron**
20ml **Lemon Juice**
10ml **Simple Syrup**

Grab your shot glass, rub some lemon along the rim, then dip into the sugar (little tip, pour the sugar into a saucer first). Fill a shaker with ice cubes, then pour in the Absolut Citron, lemon juice and simple syrup, and shake your heart out. Strain into the prepared shot glass.

HOW-TO-MIX VIDEO

VODKA SOUR

Egg white in a cocktail? It might seem strange until you try it: it adds beautiful texture to this super-tasty combination of vodka, fresh lemon and sugar. Create a sour with pretty much any spirit for a classic tart cocktail: making them at home is a life skill.

Ice Cubes
45ml **Absolut Vodka**
30ml **Lemon Juice**
15ml **Simple Syrup**
3 Dashes **Bitters**
15ml **Egg White**
1 **Lemon Zest**
1 Wedge **Lemon**
1 Whole **Cherry**

Grab a shaker and add all the liquid ingredients with ice cubes. Shake, then strain out the ice and shake again without it — don't skimp on the shaking, you need to be vigorous for a deliciously foamy top. Pour into a rocks glass filled with ice. Squeeze your lemon zest over the top of the drink before garnishing with a lemon wedge and a cherry on top.

HOW-TO-MIX VIDEO

GOOD DILL HUNTING

The key ingredient here is kümmel, an intense German liqueur flavoured with caraway, fennel and cumin. Think of this as the long-lost cousin of a Vodka Martini (page 56) — and you're ready for it.

Ice Cubes
10ml **Kümmel**
15ml **Lillet Blanc**
45ml **Absolut Vodka**
1 Twist **Lemon Zest**

Add the ice cubes, kümmel, Lillet Blanc and vodka to a mixing glass and stir until well blended and ice-cold. Strain into a chilled cocktail glass before twisting a piece of lemon zest over the drink, making sure all the delicious oils spray onto the surface. Discard the zest once that's done, but you can also drop it in the drink if you'd like to add a pop of colour.

HOW-TO-MIX VIDEO

SMOKED PINEAPPLE

Smoky, sweet, herbal, tropical... There's a lot going on in this cocktail, but it's worth putting in the effort. The smokiness comes from the whisky, so be sure to get a peated one. This one has 'special occasion' written all over it: pick a moment to savour.

½ **Lemon**
1 Thick Slice **Pineapple**
6 Leaves **Sage**
20ml **Simple Syrup**
50ml **Absolut Vodka**
Crushed Ice
4 Dashes **Peated Whisky**
1 Sprig **Sage**

Cut half a lemon into small pieces, then roughly cut the fresh pineapple into six pieces. Keep one piece of pineapple aside for garnish. Put the lemon and pineapple pieces into a rocks glass along with the sage leaves and the simple syrup. Muddle everything together in the glass until you get a pulp-like consistency, then add the vodka. Fill the glass with crushed ice and give it all a good stir. Before serving, add four dashes of smoky peated whisky, top up with crushed ice, then garnish with a sprig of sage and the remaining pineapple. What's not to love?!

HOW-TO-MIX VIDEO

APPLETINI

This genuine classic takes you back to the 90s, and who doesn't feel the need to do that now and again? The apple juice and apple liqueur bond into something light, breezy and fun. Get creative with the apple garnish, too — a fan will look particularly cool. In a 90s way, of course.

Ice Cubes
45ml **Absolut Vodka**
20ml **Lemon Juice**
25ml **Apple Liqueur**
25ml **Apple Juice**
20ml **Simple Syrup**
1 Slice **Apple**

Fill a shaker with ice cubes, pour in all the liquid ingredients and give it a really good shake. Double-strain and pour into a chilled martini glass, then garnish with the apple slice.

HOW-TO-MIX VIDEO

DORIS ROYALE

The unique gentian and vegetal notes of Suze balance with the herbal and subtle floral flavours of Lillet Blanc, and everything is elevated by the Absolut Vodka. This is a fancy drink for a fancy time, so for extra pizzazz, we finish it with champagne.

2½cm Piece **Cucumber**
25ml **Lemon Juice**
10ml **Lillet Blanc**
10ml **Suze**
20ml **Simple Syrup**
45ml **Absolut Vodka**
Ice Cubes
Champagne
1 Sprig **Mint**

Roughly chop the cucumber, then muddle it in a shaker with the lemon juice. Pour in the Lillet Blanc, Suze, simple syrup and vodka, then pack with ice cubes before giving it a good shake. Shake and double-strain into a wine glass filled with ice before topping with champagne. Garnish with a small sprig of mint for a little fresh colour.

HOW-TO-MIX VIDEO

BURNT TOASTED ALMOND

The name gives you a big clue as to what you're getting here, but it's way more than just almond. Smooth, harmonious Absolut vodka, cream and Kahlúa coffee liqueur make this is a rich, luxurious and indulgent cocktail to cap off an evening.

Ice Cubes
20ml **Amaretto**
20ml **Absolut Vodka**
30ml **Double Cream**
10ml **Cream Liqueur**
10ml **Kahlúa**
Chopped Almonds or **Ground Cinnamon (optional)**

Fill a shaker with ice cubes, then add all the ingredients except the almonds and cinnamon. Shake until nice and cold before straining into a cocktail glass. Deliciously easy. Garnish with chopped almonds or ground cinnamon.

BEVERLY HILLS ICED TEA

This one takes the iconic Long Island Iced Tea (page 40) all the way over to the West Coast for a million-dollar glow-up. Less is more with three spirits instead of the usual five, and it's topped with champagne instead of cola. Now that's glamour, baby.

Ice Cubes
15ml **Absolut Vodka**
20ml **Lime Juice**
15ml **Gin**
15ml **Simple Syrup**
25ml **Triple Sec**
Champagne
1 Wheel **Lime**

Fill a shaker with ice cubes, then pour in the vodka, lime juice, gin, simple syrup and triple sec. Give it a good shake to combine all the flavours, then strain into a wine glass filled with ice cubes. Top up with champagne and garnish with a lime wheel for an extra burst of citrus freshness.

FUSS-FREE CROWD PLEASERS

MOSCOW MULE

Fresh, fiery ginger with a good squeeze of vitalizing lime and the distinctive flavours from the winter wheat in Absolut vodka — this is a three-ingredient cocktail that's way more than the sum of its parts. It was originally created via a bit of entrepreneurial ingenuity: a vodka salesman and a ginger beer salesman came up with it in a bar one night as a way to sell more of their products, and the rest is delicious history. A true worldwide classic.

Ice Cubes
45ml **Absolut Vodka**
15ml **Lime Juice**
Ginger Beer
1 Wedge **Lime**

Fill a glass — or a stainless steel or copper mule mug if you have one — with ice cubes. Add the vodka and lime juice and stir, then top up with ginger beer. Garnish with a lime wedge.

HOW-TO-MIX VIDEO

PORNSTAR HIGHBALL

The Pornstar Martini (page 46) is one of the best-loved cocktails in the world, and here's a way to enjoy its extrovert fruitiness in a more laidback package. In this version, the all-natural bourbon vanilla characteristics of Absolut Vanilia are still there making magic with the tropical passionfruit, and the sparkling wine makes it last even longer.

30ml **Absolut Vanilia**
15ml **Simple Syrup**
15ml **Lemon Juice**
70ml **Passion Fruit Juice**
Ice Cubes
Sparkling Wine
1 Wedge **Pineapple**

Grab a highball glass, then pour in the Absolut Vanilia, simple syrup, lemon juice and passion fruit juice. Give it a good stir and fill with ice cubes. Top up with sparkling wine and garnish with the pineapple wedge.

LONG COSMOPOLITAN

The original Cosmopolitan (page 38) is a sophisticated A-lister of a cocktail that's guaranteed to enliven any evening occasion; now here's its laidback little sister, who's just as happy having a chilled night in as she is hitting the town. In other words, this still has the zesty natural lemon of Absolut Citron, but it's all layered and lengthened into an easy-to-mix highball.

45ml **Absolut Citron**
25ml **Triple Sec**
5ml **Simple Syrup**
Ice Cubes
120ml **Cranberry Juice**
1 Wedge **Orange**

Pour the Absolut Citron, triple sec and simple syrup into a highball glass and give it a good stir. Now fill to the top with ice cubes before adding the cranberry juice. Little tip: it helps to add the ice before topping the drink off so it doesn't splash or spill over. Garnish with an orange wedge.

HOW-TO-MIX VIDEO

BLACK RUSSIAN

This twist on the White Russian leaves out the cream to let the coffee liqueur mingle with the hints of caramel and vanilla in the Absolut vodka. It was invented in 1949 by a Belgian barman — we raise a glass to him.

Ice Cubes
30ml **Absolut Vodka**
30ml **Kahlúa**
1 Whole **Cherry**

Fill a rocks glass with ice cubes, then add the vodka and Kahlúa. Give it a little stir, then garnish with a cherry and get sipping!

HOW-TO-MIX VIDEO

BLOODY MARY

It might have a reputation as a hangover cure, but we think this all-time classic tastes great anytime. If you're planning a long and lazy brunch, the Bloody Mary is essential. Every bartender has their own recipe, but this one has all the right elements — the spices, the sharp tomato juice, the burst of lemon, and the smooth Absolut vodka — all in perfect balance.

Ice Cubes
45ml **Absolut Vodka**
150ml **Tomato Juice**
4 Dashes **Hot Sauce**
10ml **Worcestershire Sauce**
15ml **Lemon Juice**
1 Wedge **Lemon**
1 Stick **Celery**
1 Pinch **Ground Black Pepper**
1 Pinch **Garlic Salt**

Fill a shaker with ice cubes and pour in the vodka, tomato juice, hot sauce, Worcestershire sauce and lemon juice. Stir, or pour the contents from one end of the shaker to the other (a technique called rolling), to get it ice cold. Pour into a highball glass filled with ice and garnish with the lemon wedge and celery stick. Finish with a grind of pepper and a pinch of garlic salt.

HOW-TO-MIX VIDEO

VODKA SODA

Get the measurements just so on this one and you'll discover
a simple, sparkling way to enjoy Absolut Vodka: slight hints of
caramel and vanilla are there, followed by a fresh and fruity finish.

Ice Cubes
40ml **Absolut Vodka**
150ml **Soda Water**
15ml **Freshly Squeezed Lime Juice**
1–2 Wheels **Lime**

This one is as easy as it gets: fill a highball glass with ice cubes,
then add the vodka, soda and freshly squeezed lime juice before
garnishing with a lime wheel or two.

TIP

You can follow the same recipe
and substitute in the mixer of
your choice - like cola, ginger ale,
lemon-lime soda or tonic.

—

VODKA BRAMBLE

The Gin Bramble is a modern classic from the 1980s, and our vodka-based twist is a delicious way to make the most of the blackberries that come into season in late summer. It also looks like a ten-out-of-ten stunner, with the deep, rich red of the berries mingling with the clear vodka and lemon juice.

Crushed Ice
30ml **Absolut Vodka**
20ml **Lemon Juice**
10ml **Simple Syrup**
10ml **Créme De Mure**
2 Whole **Blackberries**

Fill a rocks glass with crushed ice and add the vodka, lemon juice and simple syrup. Give it a little stir, then add more crushed ice to make a little dome and drizzle the créme de mure around it to get the bleeding effect. Garnish with the blackberries and enjoy. So easy, so very delicious.

ELDERFLOWER COLLINS

What is it about elderflower that just says summer? Floral and elegant with an almost tropical scent that's given a sky-high boost by the Absolut vodka in this delightful highball. Nobody could say no if you bring a tray of these out at a sunny drinks party. Try it.

Ice Cubes
45ml **Absolut Vodka**
30ml **Lemon Juice**
15ml **Elderflower Cordial**
150ml **Soda Water**
2 Wheels **Lemon**

Fill a highball glass with ice, then pour in the vodka, lemon juice and elderflower cordial. Give it a stir before topping with soda water and adding a little colour with the lemon wheels to garnish.

HOW-TO-MIX VIDEO

FIREWORK

An original cocktail created for Independence Day in the US, the Firework is a simple and refreshing star-spangled celebration. Absolut Vodka united with zingy lemonade and iced tea — it's a sublime mix.

45ml **Absolut Vodka**
60ml **Iced Tea**
Ice Cubes
60ml **Lemonade**
1 Wedge **Lime**

Grab a highball glass and pour in the vodka and iced tea. Add ice, then top with the lemonade. Garnish with a lime wedge for a flash of colour. It's as easy as that!

HOW-TO-MIX VIDEO

VODKA LIME

One of the quickest and easiest drinks you can make at home — all this one needs is a good lime cordial, which will then be elevated to dizzying new heights by the Absolut Vodka.

Ice Cubes
45ml **Absolut Vodka**
40ml **Lime Cordial**
1 Wheel **Lime**

Fill a rocks glass with ice cubes, then pour in the vodka and lime cordial. Give it a little stir and finish with a lime wheel garnish.

HOW-TO-MIX VIDEO

SEA BREEZE

Here's a next-level vodka and cranberry, where the grapefruit adds an extra layer of sharpness that combines beautifully with the tart cranberry. The Sea Breeze should be a staple in your home mixing arsenal — it's straightforward but delicate and delicious.

Ice Cubes
45ml **Absolut Vodka**
80ml **Grapefruit Juice**
45ml **Cranberry Juice**
1 Wheel **Lime**

This one is quick and easy, and made in the glass. Fill a highball glass with the ice, add the vodka, cranberry juice and grapefruit juice before garnishing with a lime wheel.

YELLOWHAMMER

The undisputed home of the Yellowhammer is a bar in Tuscaloosa, which serves gallons of this cocktail when the University of Alabama's football team is playing. Not a sports fan, huh? No problem — this is just a real crowd pleaser for times that call for something punchy but fruity. It's a local legend that went global.

Ice Cubes
15ml **Absolut Vodka**
15ml **Light Rum**
15ml **Amaretto**
30ml **Orange Juice**
60ml **Pineapple Juice**
1 Slice **Orange** or 1 **Maraschino Cherry**

Fill a highball glass with ice cubes and throw in all the liquid ingredients. Stir generously before garnishing with an orange slice, or a cherry if you prefer.

HOW-TO-MIX VIDEO

VODKA CRANBERRY

So simple, but so good: the exceptionally smooth Absolut Vodka is a perfect partner to the bright, tart juice.

Ice Cubes
45ml **Absolut Vodka**
150ml **Cranberry Juice**
1 Wheel **Lime**

Fill a highball glass with ice cubes, add the vodka and cranberry juice, then finish with a lime wheel. It's as easy as 1-2-3.

HOW-TO-MIX VIDEO

CITRON LEMONADE

This mix takes a standard vodka and lemonade and gives it a citrus-charged transformation with Absolut Citron, which is made with natural flavours of lemon and a hint of lime, combining to make something truly fabulous. When life hands you lemons, you know what to do.

Ice Cubes
45ml **Absolut Citron**
120ml **Lemonade**
Soda Water
1 Wedge **Lemon**

Fill a highball glass with as much ice as it will hold, then pour in the Absolut Citron and lemonade. Top up with soda water and garnish with a lemon wedge.

HOW-TO-MIX VIDEO

RASPBERRI COLLINS

It's a little bit sour, a little bit tart, a little bit sweet — this is your ideal drink for a sun-splashed summer garden. All the wild, sun-ripened raspberry flavours of the Absolut Raspberri come through and make those fresh raspberries taste even raspberrier — It's a word, trust us.

45ml **Absolut Raspberri**
25ml **Simple Syrup**
25ml **Lemon Juice**
7 Whole **Raspberries**
Soda Water

Fill a shaker with ice cubes, the add the lemon juice, 5 raspberries, the simple syrup and the Absolut Raspberri. Give it a vigorous shake to break down the raspberries to a pulp and combine all the flavours nicely. We don't want those pesky raspberry bits in the drink, so double-strain into your highball glass filled with ice. Top with soda water and finish with a couple more raspberries.

HOW-TO-MIX VIDEO

DIRTY SHIRLEY

Time for a cocktail history lesson. The first ever mocktail was named after Hollywood's most famous child actor of the 1930s and was a craze of the time. This is her all grown up: it became New York City's summer drink of choice in 2022, and if you make, one you'll see why. Fruity, colourful and tangy. To take this drink to a whole new level, make your own grenadine — learn how on page 33.

Ice Cubes
45ml **Absolut Vodka**
10ml **Grenadine**
Ginger Ale
1 **Maraschino Cherry**

Fill a highball glass with ice cubes, then pour in the vodka and grenadine. Top up with ginger ale and finish it off with a maraschino cherry. It's as easy at that!

HOW-TO-MIX VIDEO

RASPBERRI SUNRISE

The Tequila Sunrise is a classic, but classics are there to be messed around with, and here's a twist you'll love. Despite the name, this cocktail is more suited to a relaxed sundowner. If you're still partying at sunrise, we salute you — but you should probably go to bed now.

Ice Cubes
45ml **Absolut Raspberri**
150ml **Orange Juice**
1 Dash **Grenadine**
1 Wedge **Orange**
1 Whole **Raspberry**

Fill a highball glass with ice cubes, then add the Absolut Raspberri, orange juice and a dash of grenadine for that sunset effect in the bottom of the glass. Finish by garnishing with an orange wedge and a raspberry.

HOW-TO-MIX VIDEO

GRENADINE FIZZ

A super-simple drink for those times you want something bright and breezy to enhance any occasion. Basically, it's a Vodka Collins blushed with grenadine, which adds a pretty colour and a subtle taste. Top tip: make your own grenadine for that fresh pomegranate flavour (page 33).

45ml **Absolut Vodka**
30ml **Lemon Juice**
25ml **Grenadine**
Ice Cubes
Soda Water
1 Sprig **Mint**
1 Wedge **Lemon**

Grab a highball glass and pour in the vodka, grenadine, and lemon juice. Add as much ice as the glass will hold, then top up with soda water before bringing in some fresh colour with a mint and lemon garnish.

HOW-TO-MIX VIDEO

WHITE RUSSIAN

Thanks to a certain 1998 cult hit about a bowling-loving slacker, the White Russian is one of the most famous movie cocktails ever. The main character loved these concoctions almost as much as he loved bowling. It's a sister cocktail to the Black Russian (page 92), but the layer of cream on top makes it silkier and more opulent.

Ice Cubes
40ml **Absolut Vodka**
40ml **Kahlúa**
40ml **Double Cream**

Fill a rocks glass with ice cubes, then add the vodka and Kahlúa. Top off with cream for that sumptuous layered, silky finish. Top tip: pour the cream over the back of a spoon for that beautiful layered look that will get everyone salivating.

HOW-TO-MIX VIDEO

C.R.E.A.M

Doesn't sweetened condensed milk make everything taste like a treat? This is a crowd-friendly, delicious and creamy dessert shot that'll keep everyone sweet.

30ml **Absolut Vodka**
15ml **Milk**
25ml **Sweetened Condensed Milk**

Pour all the ingredients in an ice-filled shaker, then shake until the shaker is cold. Double-strain into your shot glasses.

PINEAPPLE MARTINI

In the 1990s, cocktails were all about laidback fun, which makes anything from that golden era perfect for an easy night in. Fruit-centric martinis really came of age back then, and this version turns the already heroic pineapple into a total legend.

40ml **Absolut Vodka**
50ml **Pineapple Juice**
Ice Cubes
1 Wedge **Pineapple**

Add vodka and pineapple juice to a shaker and pack to the top with ice. Shake vigorously to get a frothy head on the pineapple juice and get it nice and cold. Double-strain into a chilled cocktail glass to get any last shards of ice out (this will avoid diluting the drink). Finish with a pineapple wedge for a tropical touch.

HOW-TO-MIX VIDEO

SUMMER SIPPERS

FLUFFY WATERMELON

Whizzing up a fresh fruit cocktail using juice from a centrifugal juicer is one way to elevate a drink into something extra alluring. Aerating juice gives it a pleasingly fluffy, frothy texture, and it also enhances the aroma and fresh flavours, making drinks like these perfect for delighting your guests at any outdoor social.

Ice Cubes
45ml **Absolut Vodka**
150ml **Watermelon Juice**
1 Slice **Watermelon**

Fill a long glass with ice, then pour in the vodka and top with the fresh watermelon juice. Garnish with a refreshing slice of watermelon.

TIP

Keen to experiment? Try putting fresh oranges, grapefruits or pineapple in your centrifugal juicer instead of the watermelon.

—

LONG ESPRESSO

An adult iced coffee for those hot days when a steaming mug of joe is not on the agenda. We've dialled down the liquor in this one to keep the ABV low, making it a beautiful daytime sipper.

Ice Cubes
25ml **Absolut Vanilia**
75ml **Cold Filter Coffee**
5ml **Kahlúa**

This is a really easy 'build in the glass' recipe, so grab a highball glass and fill it with ice cubes. Add the Kahlúa, Absolut Vanilia, stir, then top off with the cold coffee. Get sipping!

HOW-TO-MIX VIDEO

BANANA CRUSH

Vodka, banana and cream — this short but very fun take on an adult milkshake will have you smiling at its sheer joyfulness. Even better, it's no sweat to make and uses ingredients most of us have lying around the kitchen. Experiment by adding chocolate or cinnamon — go nuts! (Yes, you can add nuts too.)

½ **Banana**
Ice Cubes
45ml **Absolut Vodka**
15ml **Vanilla Syrup**
25ml **Double Cream**
25ml **Milk**
Crushed Ice
Slices **Banana**

In a shaker, muddle half a banana, then fill the shaker with ice cubes and add all the liquid ingredients. Shake well, then double-strain into a rocks glass filled with crushed ice. Place a few slices of banana on top to finish.

FROZEN APPLE

Frozen drinks are the fun drinks. When the sun is shining and there's a party on the horizon, they just seem like a really good idea. This one tastes like biting into a fresh, juicy green apple.

1 Handful **Ice Cubes**
40ml **Absolut Vodka**
10ml **Calvados**
20ml **Lime Juice**
25ml **Simple Syrup**
50ml **Apple Juice**
1 Slice **Apple**

This is a 'one step' drink, so couldn't be easier. Add a handful of ice to the blender, then add all the liquid ingredients and blend for that slushy consistency. Pour into a wine glass and garnish with a slice of apple.

TIP

If too watery add more ice cubes into the blender until desired consistency.

—

CRANBERRY PUNCH

Infusing vodka is a straightforward technique, but you'll usually have to plan it in advance. Not with this recipe — the infusion is almost instant. With this simple technique, you can pack in a load of flavour, quickly. Don't confuse simple for plain, though — it's a complex-tasting little number.

Ice Cubes
25ml **Cranberry-Infused Absolut Vodka (see below)**
25ml **Lime Juice**
25ml **Lillet Rosé**
25ml **Simple Syrup**
Soda Water
1 Sprig **Rosemary**

For the Cranberry-Infused Absolut Vodka
1 x 700ml or 750ml Bottle **Absolut Vodka**
100g **Frozen Cranberries**

To infuse the vodka, combine the Absolut Vodka and frozen cranberries in a blender and blend for 1 minute. Fine-strain, then bottle. Fill a rocks glass with ice cubes. Add the infused vodka and all other liquid ingredients. Stir, then garnish with a rosemary sprig.

—

MONDAY IN MARRAKECH

It may seem strange to see lemon juice and vanilla ice cream together in a cocktail, but trust us on this one — it's another frozen banger. It's as easy as pie to make and tastes just like a lemon cream pie.

Handful of **Ice Cubes**
45ml **Absolut Vodka**
30ml **Lemon Juice**
20ml **Simple Syrup**
1 Large Scoop **Vanilla Ice Cream**

Combine all the ingredients in a blender and blend until everything is beautifully combined. Pour into a tall glass, or dress it up in a sundae glass.

TIP

If too watery add more ice cubes into the blender until desired consistency.

—

WATERMELON SMASH

A Smash is a historic cocktail dating back to the mid-19th century, and usually involves some kind of fruit, mint leaves and a spirit, all coming together into a no-nonsense, good-times drink that's begging to be smashed out on a sunny day. Our version uses juicy, sweet watermelon — if there was an official fruit of summer, this would be it, no contest.

2 Wedges **Watermelon**
Ice Cubes
50ml **Absolut Vodka**
20ml **Simple Syrup**
20ml **Lime Juice**
Ice Cubes

Muddle 1 wedge of watermelon with the simple syrup in a shaker. Add ice cubes and all the liquid ingredients before shaking to chill. Strain into a rocks glass filled with ice. For the ultimate taste of summer, garnish with the remaining watermelon wedge.

VODKA MOJITO

Okay, people: it's lime time. As with the original rum Mojito, this is a fiesta of mouth-pleasing lime, mint, and soda water. Sub out rum for the complimentary smooth experience of Absolut Vodka and a refreshing drink that hits the spot for any outdoor occasion.

6 Whole **Mint Leaves**
1 **Lime, Quartered**
20ml **Simple Syrup**
Crushed Ice
45ml **Absolut Vodka**
Soda Water
1 Sprig **Mint**

Add the lime and simple syrup to a highball glass and muddle. Then add the mint and fill the glass with crushed ice. Add the vodka and stir. Finally, top up with soda water before garnishing with a small sprig of mint.

MANGO DELIGHT

We just can't stop giving you frozen delights. This one is made with fresh mango, and there's nothing better for the summertime. It's sweet and tropical with some serious beachside vibes.

1 Handful **Ice Cubes**
45ml **Absolut Vodka**
20ml **Lime Juice**
20ml **Simple Syrup**
2 Slices **Mango**

Add a handful of ice to a blender before adding the rest of the ingredients, except for one of the mango slices. Blend to combine all the flavours into a delicious slush before pouring into a wine glass. Garnish with a mango slice.

TIP

If you really love mango, add more!

HAWAIIAN COSMOPOLITAN

If the classic Cosmopolitan (page 38) is a nightclub drink, then the Hawaiian Cosmopolitan is a dayclub drink — laidback and carefree, perfect for a long summer day. A sunny garden, a speaker and a hot playlist make a pretty good dayclub substitute, so long as you've got a Hawaiian Cosmo at the ready.

Ice Cubes
45ml **Absolut Vodka**
15ml **Triple Sec**
10ml **Lime Juice**
5ml **Simple Syrup**
40ml **Pineapple Juice**
1 wedge **Pineapple**

Fill a shaker with ice cubes, then add all the liquid ingredients. Give it a good shake to combine all the beautiful flavours and get it nice and cold before straining into a cocktail glass. Garnish with a pineapple wedge.

TIP

Juice your own pineapple or muddle one slice (without the core) to really elevate this recipe.

SUMMERTIME COOKOUT

A super-light, spirit-forward Old Fashioned variation, with the flowery scent and exotic fruit flavours of Lillet Rosé carried skywards by Absolut Vodka until they meet the zesty, sunny grapefruit. If you're already dreaming of this summer's first barbecue, don't dream any more — find some coals, grab the ingredients for this little beauty and get out there.

Ice Cubes
5ml **Simple Syrup**
13ml **Lillet Rosé**
4 Dashes **Grapefruit Bitters**
45ml **Absolut Vodka**
1 Twist **Grapefruit Zest**

Fill a mixing glass with ice cubes, then pour in the simple syrup, Lillet Rosé, grapefruit bitters and vodka. Stir to chill, then strain into a rocks glass filled with ice cubes. Garnish with the grapefruit zest and remember to squeeze those delicious oils onto the surface of the drink before dropping it in.

HOW-TO-MIX VIDEO

VODKA BASIL SMASH

Some classic cocktails go back over 100 years, but here's a modern classic from 2008 that has still managed to conquer the world. The original was invented in Hamburg and used gin, but we think the Absolut Vodka lets the distinctive basil flavours shine through. If it's summertime, keep it light, keep it herbal: the Vodka Basil Smash is ideal.

15 Leaves **Basil**
20ml **Lemon Juice**
10ml **Simple Syrup**
45ml **Absolut Vodka**
Ice Cubes

Gently muddle all but one of the basil leaves with the lemon juice in a shaker. Smash them together to draw out that powerful fresh basil taste. Add the simple syrup and vodka, then top up with lots and lots of ice. Shake vigorously to chill before double-straining into a rocks glass filled with ice. Finish it off with your best-looking basil leaf.

HOW-TO-MIX VIDEO

BAY OF PASSION

If we were to sum up this cocktail in one word, it would be 'exotic'. That's because of the fragrant passion fruit liqueur and the sweet, tart pineapple, which are optimised by the Absolut vodka. Can we have one more word? 'Delicious'. That's it. Your next outdoor party needs this.

Ice Cubes
30ml **Absolut Vodka**
15ml **Passion Fruit Liqueur**
50ml **Cranberry Juice**
50ml **Pineapple Juice**
1 Wheel **Lime**

Fill a highball glass with ice cubes before adding all your liquid ingredients. Finish it off with a zesty lime wheel and get sipping!

TIP

To give this drink a lovely fluffy texture, make your own pineapple juice using a centrifugal juicer.

—

RASPBERRI RASPIROSKA

Here's something light, fresh-tasting and cold you can sip during an afternoon outside, no stress. It's built in the glass, so there's no need for any special equipment, and it's bursting with the fresh fruit flavours and intense berry aroma of Absolut Raspberri.

7 Whole **Raspberries**
20ml **Simple Syrup**
Crushed Ice
45ml **Absolut Raspberri**
20ml **Lime Juice**

Gently muddle all but one of the raspberries and the simple syrup in a rocks glass. Fill the glass with crushed ice then add the Absolut Raspberri and lime juice. Garnish with the remaining raspberry, and you're all set.

LYCHEE COOLER

How do you make a Lychee Cooler? Put a pair of sunglasses on it. Sorry. Now we've got that out of the way, here's the drink: a cooler is a cousin of the spritz, and it's everything you want in a summertime party drink. This one is sweet, delicate, sparkling and pretty, with aromatic lychee and exceptionally smooth Absolut Vodka.

Ice Cubes
20ml **Absolut Vodka**
20ml **Lychee Liqueur**
5ml **Simple Syrup**
150ml **Sparkling Wine**
1 Whole, Peeled **Lychee**

Fill a shaker with ice cubes, then add the vodka, lychee liqueur and simple syrup. Give it a good shake to combine all the delicious flavours before double-straining into a wine glass. Last but not least, add the sparkling wine and garnish with a lychee.

RASPBERRY BLIMEY

If the Raspberri Raspiroska (page 156) is berry good, this one is berry *berry* good. It's similar, but the blackcurrant liqueur adds another layer of flavour, making it richer, darker and a little more complex. Bust this one out when the sun's going down but the party's not ready to end just yet.

6 Whole **Raspberries**
10ml **Blackcurrant Liqueur**
10ml **Lime Juice**
10ml **Simple Syrup**
Crushed Ice
45ml **Absolut Vodka**
1 Whole **Blackberry**

This is a built drink, made directly in a rocks glass. Begin by muddling all but one of the raspberries with the blackcurrant liqueur, lime juice and simple syrup together. Next, fill the glass with crushed ice, then pour in the vodka and give it a good stir. Bring a final touch of colour by garnishing with the remaining raspberry and a blackberry.

SWEDISH SPRITZ

In the north of Sweden, the sun barely sets in the summer. We understand that in other parts of the world, you need to make the most of every break in the clouds, so here's a drink to celebrate summer wherever you are. Savoury ingredients make this a unique drink, and the Absolut Citron makes it bright with a burst of lemon.

Ice Cubes
30ml **Absolut Citron**
15ml **Fino Sherry**
2 Dashes **Cucumber Bitters**
Elderflower Tonic
1 Sprig **Dill**
1 Slice **Cucumber**
1 Slice **Strawberry**

Fill a wine glass with ice cubes and add the Absolut Citron, fino sherry and cucumber bitters. Stir well before topping up with elderflower tonic. Finish with a classic Swedish garnish: a sprig of dill, a slice of cucumber and a piece of juicy strawberry.

PIÑA

An easy-pouring, easy-sipping summer gem: smooth
Absolut Vodka starts a party with vibrantly sweet pineapple
and you're invited.

Ice Cubes
45ml **Absolut Vodka**
150ml **Pineapple Juice**
1 Wedge **Pineapple**

This is an easy one: fill a highball glass with ice cubes, then
add the vodka and pineapple juice, before garnishing with a
pineapple wedge.

TIP

Want to impress your friends?
Juice your own pineapple and
maybe even give the drink a
little shake. Trust us, they will not
believe it's just pineapple in there.

SWEETHEART

The Italian tradition of aperitivo — a drink designed to get your appetite firing before a meal — is one we should frankly all get on board with. The Sweetheart is a little tart, a little bitter, a little sweet, and totally *bellissimo*. Kick off your next dinner party with some Italian flair!

Ice Cubes
20ml **Absolut Vodka**
20ml **Aperol**
20ml **Cranberry Juice**
5ml **Limoncello**
5ml **Lemon Juice**
3 Whole **Cranberries** or 1 Twist **Lemon Zest**

Fill a shaker with ice cubes. Add all the liquid ingredients, then shake and strain into a rocks glass filled with ice cubes. Garnish with cranberries or a lemon zest twist, if you can't find cranberries.

ALIGATORADE

There's no added sugar in this high-summer sipper — so make it when you want something naturally sweet and a bit lower in alcohol with a refreshing taste. Absolut Citron is the star of the show here: its fresh, citrussy character and note of lemon peel add a ray of sunshine to any summer occasion.

1 Slice **Pineapple**
20ml **Lime Juice**
90ml **Coconut Water**
45ml **Absolut Citron**
3 Dashes **Bitters**
Ice Cubes
1 **Pineapple Leaf**

Grab a shaker, and start by muddling the pineapple slice into a pulp (just use the flesh and remove the core). Add the lime juice, coconut water, Absolut Citron and bitters and fill the shaker with ice cubes before giving it a good shake to combine those tropical flavours. Double-strain into a rocks glass over ice and garnish with a pineapple leaf.

HOW-TO-MIX
VIDEO

HOLIDAY FAVOURITES

PUMPKIN PIE MARTINI

Piles of fallen leaves, a drift of wood smoke, Halloween costumes for your pet — some things just shout autumn. You can add spiced pumpkin pie to that list, and here's the drinkable version of that dessert. Wrap up warm, gather your people and get cosy with a cocktail (yes, this is real proof that cocktails can be cosy).

Ice Cubes
45ml **Absolut Vanilia**
15ml **Cinnamon Syrup**
30ml **Milk**
30ml **Pumpkin Purée**

Pack a shaker with ice cubes, then add all the ingredients. Shake well to combine all the flavours before straining into a cocktail glass.

APPLE PIE SHOT

Apple, cinnamon and vanilla — an all-time classic flavour combination that somehow becomes even tastier in autumn. Apologies if you have an uncontrollable craving for a slice of actual pie after this, but that's just how good it is. Here's your Friendsgiving party starter.

1 Wedge **Lemon**
Caster Sugar
Ground Cinnamon
Ice Cubes
30ml **Absolut Vanilia**
20ml **Apple Juice**
10ml **Lemon Juice**
10ml **Simple Syrup**
1 Slice **Apple**

Start by preparing your shot glass: run a lemon wedge around the rim and dip the rim of the glass into a saucer of sugar mixed with cinnamon. Next, grab a shaker, pack it with ice cubes and add all the liquid ingredients. Shake well and strain into your prepared shot glass. Garnish with an apple slice and serve.

HOW-TO-MIX VIDEO

HOLLIS

Looking for a jolly Christmas drink? You can do better than that tired old bottle of sherry at the back of the cabinet, trust us. The Hollis is strong, gently spiced, alcohol-forward and totally indulgent — perfect for sipping beside a crackling fire while opening your presents.

Ice Cubes
45ml **Absolut Vodka**
25ml **Lillet Rouge**
5ml **Rich Syrup**
4 Drops **Chocolate Bitters**
1 Twist **Orange Zest**

Start by filling a mixing glass with ice cubes, then add vodka, Lillet Rouge, rich syrup and chocolate bitters. Stir until beautifully combined and nicely chilled. Strain and pour into a rocks glass filled with ice, then garnish with a twist of orange zest, not forgetting to squeeze those delicious oils over the surface of the drink first.

HOW-TO-MIX VIDEO

HOLIDAY MULE

Basically, this is like a classic Moscow Mule, but with a snuggly scarf and rosy cheeks. Apple cider and spiced ginger are elevated by Absolut Vodka into a seasonal drink that's made for bringing people together. Get them going for Thanksgiving.

Ice Cubes
45ml **Absolut Vodka**
40ml **Apple Cider of Choice**
40ml **Ginger Beer**
10ml **Lemon Juice**
1 Slice/Wheel **Apple**
1 Stick **Cinnamon**

Fill a highball glass with ice cubes, then pour in all the liquid ingredients. Give it a quick stir before finishing off with a slice/ wheel of apple and a cinnamon stick.

HIGHROLLER

If there's ever a time to go big with the cocktails, it's the holiday season. And this pared-back stunner brings together two quality bottles in style — exceptionally smooth and balanced Absolut Vodka, and crisp, beautifully effervescent champagne.
Got friends coming over for New Year's Eve drinks?
Show them how you roll.

Ice Cubes
30ml **Absolut Vodka**
Champagne

Fill a rocks glass with ice cubes, add the vodka, then top up with champagne.

COSMO CHAMPAGNE COCKTAIL

Name a celebration that isn't improved with champagne. We've got all day. And even the Cosmopolitan (page 38), that irrepressible 90s icon, gets a little bit glitzier when some good bubbly is involved. This cocktail is just perfect for a romantic Valentine's Day treat, with zesty Absolut Citron taking the leading role.

Ice Cubes
30ml **Absolut Citron**
15ml **Triple Sec**
15ml **Cranberry Juice**
8ml **Lime Juice**
Champagne
1 Spiral **Orange Peel**

Grab a shaker and pack it with ice cubes, then pour in the Absolut Citron, triple sec, cranberry juice and lime juice. Shake, then strain into a champagne glass. Finish it off by topping up with champagne and garnishing with a spiral of orange peel.

CHOCOLATE MARTINI

Everyone eats too much chocolate at Easter. It's just part of life. Give yourself a break from the chocolate eggs and shake up one of these rich, boozy and luxurious drinks instead — it's ideal for putting the cherry on a cheery festive gathering.

Ice Cubes
40ml **Absolut Vodka**
20ml **White Chocolate Liqueur**
1 **Almond**

Pack a shaker with ice cubes, then add the vodka and white chocolate liqueur. Shake well to bring all those delicious flavours together, then strain into a cocktail glass. Garnish the drink with an almond and serve with a piece of chocolate on the side.

SWEDISH DEATH NETTLE

Nettles: the scourge of bare summertime skin, but boy do they make a tasty cocktail. In Sweden, Midsummer — a celebration of the summer solstice — is a big deal, and this showstopper is our grown-up, delicious tribute to it. And is this the best name for a cocktail ever? It could well be.

Ice Cubes
25ml **Lime Juice**
20ml **Nettle Cordial**
45ml **Absolut Vodka**
50ml **Nettle Tea**
Soda Water
1 Sprig **Mint**

Fill a highball glass with ice cubes, pour in the lime juice, nettle cordial, vodka and nettle tea. Add a splash of soda water to top up, and finish with a fresh sprig of mint to garnish.

TIP

if you can't find nettle cordial and nettle tea, substitute them with elderflower cordial and green tea; it will make a very different but still delicious drink.

—

KAJU KAPI

Generally falling in October/November, the Hindu, Sikh and Jain festival of Diwali is widely celebrated in India. The warm, golden colours of marigold flowers are everywhere at this time, so honour the symbolic triumph of light over darkness and the start of the Hindu New Year with this pretty creation — the marigold syrup brings a uniquely citrussy taste with a gentle touch of bitterness. Happy Diwali!

60ml **Absolut Vodka**
30ml **Espresso**
20ml **Marigold Syrup (see below)**
20ml **Cashew Milk**
Ice Cubes
1 **Edible Flower**

For the Marigold Syrup
10g **Marigold Petals, Dried or Fresh**
300g **Sugar**

To make the marigold syrup, combine the marigold petals and 300ml hot water and leave to brew for 15 minutes. Add the sugar and stir until combined, then strain and let cool.

To make the cocktail, combine all the liquid ingredients in a shaker with ice, and shake until the flavours are blended and the liquid is chilled. Strain into a cocktail glass and garnish with an edible flower.

THANDAI HIGHBALL

The traditional highlight of the Indian festival of Holi is when everyone smears handfuls of colourful powder and splashes water at each other. You've probably seen this and thought, why aren't all celebrations this fun? A lesser-known Holi tradition is thandai, a cooling drink made with milk, saffron, spices and rose. Less messy, just as iconic.

60ml **Absolut Vodka**
10ml **Honey Syrup (see below)**
10ml **Lime Juice**
10ml **Condensed Milk**
Ice Cubes
Soda Water
1 **Almond Praline** and 1 Pinch **Saffron Strands**

For the Almond, Saffron and Cardamom Honey Syrup
150g **Toasted Chopped Almonds**
1 Pinch **Saffron Strands**
¼ Cup **Cardamom Pods**
350ml **Runny Honey**

To make the syrup, combine the almonds, saffron and cardamom with 500ml boiling water in a saucepan over a low heat. Heat gently until reduced by half. Stir in the honey, then take off the heat and leave to sit for an hour before straining.

To make the cocktail, combine the vodka, honey syrup, lime juice and condensed milk in an ice-filled shaker and shake until the shaker is cold. Fine-strain into a highball glass filled with ice, then top with soda water. Garnish with almond praline and a pinch of saffron strands.

FORTUNE TEA

Lunar New Year is the biggest holiday on the Chinese calendar, a 15-day extravaganza to usher in wealth and good fortune for the future. Get yourself some of those auspicious wishes with this Asian-style sour, where date-infused vodka blends with Chinese tea to create something fragrant and rich.

45ml **Date-Infused Absolut Vodka (see below)**
25ml **Black Tea Syrup (see below)**
30ml **Apple Juice**
30ml **Lemon Juice**
20ml **Egg White**
Ice Cubes
A Few **Crystaliized Ginger Slices**

For the Date-Infused Absolut Vodka
1 x 700ml Bottle **Absolut Vodka**
100g **Dates**

For the Black Tea Syrup
3 **Chinese Black Tea Bags** or **Black Tea Bags of Choice**
500g **Sugar**

Infuse the vodka with the dates according to the instructions on page 29, then leave to sit for 12 hours. To make the Black Tea Syrup, steep the tea bags in 500ml boiling water in a saucepan for 5 minutes. Add the sugar and heat gently until the sugar dissolves. Leave to cool. To make the cocktail, pour all the liquid ingredients into an ice-filled shaker and shake for longer than usual to blend the flavours and chill. Strain into a rocks glass with ice and garnish with a few crystallized ginger slices.

—

MOCKTAILS

RASPBERRY SPRITZER

A liquid love poem to the queen of summer fruits, with nothing more than a bit of simple syrup to bring out its rich sweetness, and sparkling soda to lengthen that crimson colour and add refreshment. (And it's easier than writing an actual love poem, because nothing rhymes with raspberry. Try it.)

Ice Cubes
7 Whole **Raspberries**
15ml **Simple Syrup**
25ml **Lemon Juice**
150ml **Soda Water**
1 Sprig **Mint**

Muddle all but two of the raspberries and simple syrup in a cocktail shaker until they are nicely mashed together, then add the lemon juice. Fill the shaker with ice and shake until cold. Double-strain into an ice-filled wine glass and top with soda water. Garnish with the remaining raspberries and a fresh sprig of mint.

VIRGIN ESPRESSO

Bitter, bold and powerful, this is a virgin cocktail that's punchy enough to perk up any get-together, and elegant enough to turn heads. That pretty layer of creamy foam on top comes from a hard shaking — put in the effort, and you'll be rewarded!

Ice Cubes
60ml **Cold Espresso**
30ml **Vanilla Syrup**
30ml **Water**
2 Whole **Coffee Beans**

Fill a shaker with ice cubes, then pour in all the liquid ingredients and shake vigorously to combine the delicious flavours. Strain into a cocktail glass, then garnish with two coffee beans.

CITRON PRESSÉ

Think of this as the best lemonade you ever had — and it's way more thoughtful than just opening a can of pop for your guests. What's more, it's simple: minimal effort on your behalf, maximum citrussy sunshine for them.

Crushed Ice
30ml **Lemon Juice**
15ml **Simple Syrup**
75ml **Soda Water**
1 Wheel **Lemon**

Fill a highball glass with crushed ice, then pour in all the liquid ingredients and stir to combine. Finish it off with a nice lemon wheel.

VIRGIN APPLETINI

The Appletini was one of the iconic drinks of the 1990s, and here's how you can get some of those fruity, flirty vibes with zero alcohol. Will it taste even better if you're wearing platform trainers and a crop top? Only you can answer that.

Ice Cubes
15ml **Lemon Juice**
15ml **Simple Syrup**
60ml **Apple Juice**
1 Slice **Apple**

Fill a shaker with ice cubes, add all the liquid ingredients and give it a good shake. Once everything is nicely combined and chilled, strain into a cocktail glass and garnish with a slice of apple.

TIP

Press your own or buy the best-quality apple juice.

—

VIRGIN MOJITO

Could this alcohol-free version of everybody's favourite Caribbean cocktail be even better than the original? Unpopular opinion, but maybe it is: because with this one, everybody gets to experience the life-changing combination of mint, sugar, lime and soda on a hot day.

45ml **Lime Juice**
6 Whole **Mint Leaves**
30ml **Simple Syrup**
Ice Cubes
Soda Water
1 Sprig **Mint**

Add the lime juice, mint leaves and simple syrup to a highball glass, then fill with ice. Top up with soda water and garnish with a sprig of mint.

HOW-TO-MIX VIDEO

INDEX

CREDITS

We would like to thank everyone that has contributed to this book — especially to Purfict for the cocktail and prop styling and to Anders Kylberg, Emil Larsson and Andreas Näslund for their photography.

Anders Kylberg: pages 41, 51, 57, 61, 67, 69, 71, 87, 91, 95, 97, 105, 107, 109 113, 115, 119, 123, 127, 133, 177
Emil Larsson: pages 39, 43, 45, 47, 49, 59, 73, 79, 93, 101, 131, 155, 157, 175, 187
Andreas Näslund: pages 53, 55, 63, 65, 75, 77, 81, 83, 89, 99, 103, 111, 117, 121, 125, 135, 137, 139, 141, 143, 145, 147, 149, 151, 153, 159, 161, 163, 165, 167, 169, 173, 179, 181, 183, 185, 189, 191, 193, 197, 199, 201, 203, 205

All recipes serve one

**This book is to be enjoyed by people over the legal drinking age.
Please remember to drink responsibly.**

Managing Director Sarah Lavelle
Senior Commissioning Editor Sophie Allen
Designer Claire Rochford
Cover Design The Mix Stockholm Creative Agency
Original recipes by Ricardo Dynan (Sit Down, Gangster, Good Dill
Hunting, Doris Royale, Summertime Cookout, Aligatorade, Hollis,
Swedish Death Nettle)
Additional Material Euan Ferguson
Drinks Styling Purfict
Photography See page 207
Head of Production Stephen Lang
Production Controller Martina Georgieva

Published in 2023 by Quadrille,
an imprint of Hardie Grant Publishing

Quadrille
52—54 Southwark Street
London SE1 1UN
quadrille.com

Cataloguing in Publication Data: a catalogue record for this book is
available from the British Library.

ISBN 978 1 83783 110 4

Printed in China

—

SKÅL!